Top 10 Baking Tips

Betty Sherman

If you're not an experienced baker, your first time making your own cookies, cake or other baked goods can be a little scary. Baking seems quite different than normal cooking. It's true that there's a learning curve to baking; however being a great baker is in many ways easier than being a great cook.

In baking, there are just a few key techniques you need to learn to be able to bake most things. With cooking, almost every dish is completely different.

Ready to learn how to create delectable cookies, heart warming cakes and goodies that friends and family will beg for? Start with these ten tips.

Tip #1: Buy an Oven Thermometer

The first thing you need to do to get your baking "career" off on the right foot is to get an oven thermometer.

Many of the ovens in today's kitchens are quite far off. If you preheat your oven to 300, you may actually be heating it to 350 or to 250. That's a very dramatic difference that will result in a dramatically different cake at the end of the day.

When you're following a recipe, you don't want variances in heat to get in the way. Don't trust your oven's temperature dials. Get an oven thermometer. They're very inexpensive and will make your life a whole lot easier.

Note: Don't get the single-use turkey baking kind. Get a sturdy oven thermometer you can use over and over again.

Tip #2: Get All Your Ingredients in One Place

This is advice you commonly see in cookbooks and recipes. It's so common, in fact, that many people start to ignore it.

With baking however, this is a crucial step. Beginning bakers will often forget one or two ingredients their first time along. In baking, timing is everything. If you suddenly realize you don't have an important ingredient the moment you need it, the whole batch could be ruined.

Don't leave your ingredients up to chance. Get everything in one place before you start. Re-read the recipe to make sure you truly have everything you need in front of you. For your first few times baking, it can also help to measure out all your ingredients before you start. That way you can focus on baking, instead of measuring ingredients once you've begun.

Tip #3: Recipe Study and Mental Runthroughs

The first time you cook a specific recipe, make it a point to read and re-read the recipe until it feels like second nature to you.

Read through each and every step of the directions and visualize them. See what the process should look like in your mind before you start baking.

Taking the time to go through this preparation process will help you get acquainted with the recipe. You'll be able to move a lot quicker once your recipe is ingrained in your mind, as opposed to having to constantly re-read passages as you bake.

Tip #4: Use Baking Sheet Lining

Line baking sheets on your kitchen counter, where you'll be placing your cutting board and ingredients. This helps flour from getting all over the place. Line your baking sheets to help prevent cookies from sticking.

Use lining generously throughout the baking process. You'll make much less of a mess, need less time for cleanup and your baked foods will come out better.

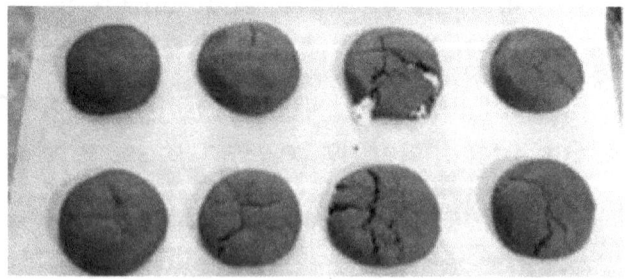

Tip #5: Don't Over Mix

In recipes, you'll often find the phrase "don't over mix." What does that actually mean?

In the last phase of making cake batter of cookie dough, you combine the dry ingredients (E.g. flour) with the wet ingredients (E.g. milk, eggs.) As soon as this happens, the flour starts to bind with the rest of the ingredients and the dough starts to form. Mixing helps this process happen.

However, if you mix the dough too much, the bond will get too strong. The cookie dough will grow tough, which will result in hard to chew cookies or brittle and dry cakes.

So what's the right amount of time to spend mixing? Mix only until the texture in the dough or batter is even. As soon as you can't see flour anymore, stop mixing.

Tip #6: Measure Ingredients Exactly

Don't just add "a pinch of sugar" or a "generous amount of milk." When you split the dough in half, don't just eyeball it.

Remember that baking is really a deliberate chemical reaction. If you want to get the same chemical reaction that another baker got, you need to use the same amount of base chemicals. In other words, your ingredients need to be exact.

Yes, seasoned bakers can just "eye it" and cook up fantastic meals. For beginning bakers who're following recipes however, exact measurement are crucial. Don't use imprecise measurements until you've baked what you're baking a few times.

Tip #7: Don't Confuse Baking Powder with Baking Soda

In normal cooking, it's not unusual to substitute one item for another. Ran out of garlic? Throw in some onions or ginger to give it some spice. In baking however, some items simply shouldn't be switched out for others.

Baking powder and baking soda are two such items. These are two very different mixtures that shouldn't be changed for one another. Doing so will easily ruin your recipe.

Baking powder is baking soda, except it has acid in it. Baking soda has no acid. These cause different reactions. It'll cause the cookies or cake to rise in different ways. Don't interchange these, or you'll get something quite different than what you expected.

Tip #8: The Perfect Time to Pull Out a Cake

Baking your cake for too long will suck the moisture right out of the mixture, resulting in a dry cake that simply doesn't taste good. You'll have wasted hours of hard work for nothing. Knowing the right moment to pull out your cake is crucial.

One simple test you can use to test whether or not the cake is ready is to stick in a small skewer. You can use thin wood skewers, glass skewers or even just toothpicks. If you see batter coming off on the skewer, it needs a bit more time. If it's just cooked crumbs and it's otherwise clean, the cake is ready.

You can also press the center of your cake with your finger. If it springs back up quickly without jiggling, it's done.

You can even test the cake by taking its temperature. A cake's internal temperature should be around 210 when it's done baking.

You should start testing the cake for doneness once you see the edge of the cake contract from the pan. In other words, when a gap starts to appear on the edge of the cake, between the cake and the pan, that's when you should start testing your cake.

Tip #9: Sift Your Dry Ingredients

Using flour that's been compressed isn't a good idea. It lumps together and creates a denser texture. Sifted flour on the other hand is airier and makes for better cookies. The same goes for other dry ingredients like baking powder, baking soda and cacao.

Don't think that just because you bought pre-sifted flour that you don't need to do any sifting. Flour has very small molecules and gets compressed very easily. Even pre-sifted flour can compact itself and get clumped up again.

Make it a habit to sift your dry ingredients before you do any baking.

Tip #10: Follow the Instructions to a T for the First time

Yes, it's true that cooking is an artistic expression. And yes, of course you'll want to add your own personalized touch to recipes.

However, the first time you bake a cake, a sheet of cookies or other goodies, avoid making any changes to the recipe. You want your first try to be a success. Modifying things can easily turn a winning recipe into a failure

If the cake doesn't come out right the first time, spend some time tweaking it until it comes out perfect. Only once you've got the original cake to come out right at least once should you start personalizing your recipe.

Learning to bake your own cookies or cakes is a fantastic way to add some sweetness to your family and your friends' lives. These 10 tips will help you create the absolutely perfect baked goods with just a little practice.

www.ingramcontent.com/pod-product-compliance
Lightning Source LLC
LaVergne TN
LVHW021751060526
838200LV00052B/3579